Inspired

My Life (so far) in Poems

Courtney Cooperman

Photography by Jodi & Courtney Cooperman

authorHOUSE®

AuthorHouse™
1663 Liberty Drive
Bloomington, IN 47403
www.authorhouse.com
Phone: 1-800-839-8640

First published by AuthorHouse   7/13/2010

ISBN: 978-1-4520-3169-9 (e)
ISBN: 978-1-4520-3168-2 (sc)

Library of Congress Control Number: 2010908347

Printed in the United States of America
Bloomington, Indiana

This book is printed on acid-free paper.

I Am . . .

I am Courtney Cooperman
I wonder about the world and its past and future
I hear my friends laughing when we have fun
I see worlds in a stack or better known as heaps of books
I am unique.

I used to pretend my dolls were alive and were my children
I feel that I can make a difference
I touch the page of a book with love
I worry of a horrible future
I cry when I am upset or have upset someone
I am a child.

I understand many Jewish customs and enjoy them
I say the world should be peaceful
I dream of a future filled with kindness
I try to help others
I hope for a happy life in which I can make a difference
I am myself.

Poetry Guide: Inspired

Seeing that word makes me think,
Inspired, inspired, inspired,
Inspired – I think I'll write a poem about that word! How will I do it? Let's see – when I
think about inspired, what do I think about? A beautiful sunset! Hmmm . . .
A beautiful sunset,
Inspiring,
Me watching one,
Inspired. Yes, a writer watching a sunset,
Inspired.

Sometimes people ask me how I write poems, this will help them understand.
A writer sees things differently from other people.
An artist sees the color in a sunset,
A scientist sees the makeup of one,
A writer sees the words in one.
Orange, pink, purple,
Gases, chemicals, heat,
Serene, unique, gorgeous, magical.
Inspired, inspired, inspired by the sunset.
Words come first and then a poem,
I'm inspired at random moments,
What a unique laugh you have! Oh, yes! I'll write a poem about laughter!
Giggle, chortle, snort,
Oh! What an odd temperature for spring! Today I'll write about the weather,
Chilly, wet, frigid.
Inspired, inspired, inspired,
By that word I am inspired.
When I think of an idea, my free time's booked,
My mind becomes full of ideas,
I am drawn to the keyboard to type this new poem,
Pulled by the power of inspired.

Foreword

Courtney started writing poetry in second grade. The first section of her book, *Primary Poems*, are poems written both in school and at home and while waiting for the food to come at the Millburn Diner...those we called, "Poems from the Diner" and they are mixed into the *Primary Poems*. As the name indicates, those were written in her primary years of elementary school. Courtney has decided to share all of her poetry, including those special and personal poems that she has written for birthdays, anniversaries and special occasions; you will certainly learn a lot about all of our lives as you read *People I Love*. Her final chapter, *Ideas and Emotions*, is truly inspirational. Her depth of understanding and compassion goes far beyond her twelve years, and this chapter will certainly leave you thinking and more importantly, inspired!

We are so proud of the time and effort she has made in organizing 5 years of poetry into this special collection as part of her mitzvah project. The profits that she makes on the sale of her book will be used to help fulfill the wishes of the students at SPARK Academy, the charter school in Newark where Courtney is dedicating countless hours of time as a homework helper for two students.

We wanted to make a special note and mention that one of her recent poems, *The Last Last Day*, was chosen by <u>Stone Soup Magazine</u> for publication, therefore it could not be published in her personal book as well. We are all very proud that her poem was accepted and will be published in the summer of 2010! We hope that you find her book inspiring.

Jodi and Wayne Cooperman
May 2010

Table of Contents

Primary Poems

Beaches

Waves, splashing on sand,
Sand is wet, good for castles,
Children having fun.

Trees

Tall, swaying beauties,
A precious sight above me,
Graceful overhead.

Cities

Noisy, busy streets,
Cars for miles and miles,
Buildings reach the sky.

Sunset

Clouds of pink,
The moon is awakening,
The sun drifts off,
Colorful sight,
Soon stars take
Over the land
Where the sun
Has once
Glowed.

Flowers

Beautiful, colorful,
Swaying, blooming, growing,
Make a rainbow garden,
Blossoms.

America

Free, united,
Helping, working, playing,
The best country ever,
U.S.A.

Spring

Flowers blooming, as if they're awaking,
The birds chirp with the breeze like they're singing,
The sky blue as the ocean waves,
With no more snow, the roads look like they've been paved!

Michelle Kwan

The thing we like about Michelle Kwan,
She is a skater and is still going on!
She started skating at a very young age,
She is the dancer; the ice is her stage!

Rainforests

Dark, misty and green,
Animals, some are unknown,
So mysterious,
Trees, for miles and miles,
A beautiful sight,
What a wonderful place.

Rosh Hashanah Symbols

A full plate of apples, all drizzled
With honey,
On some apples it sticks tight, on some
It is runny.
The challah, so round and braided so tight,
Well it is not long before the slices
Take flight.
On the holiday morning it's cheery
And bright.
And we know it is a New Year, why?
For the ram's horn's great might.

Halloween

Happy, happy, Halloween
Amazingly fun holiday
Lollipops, candy bars, and more
Lots and lots of fun for everyone
Oh, there are lots of great costumes
What a sight to see
Everybody loves Halloween
Excellent everything
Night of lots of spooky things

We love Halloween!

Halloween Night

You'll see witches,
You'll see ghosts,
You'll see spooky kinds of notes.
You'll see black cats,
Goblins too,
And maybe a spooky surprise for you!

But Halloween's not just spooks and ghosts,
It's candy corn, lollipops, coming from kind trick-or-treat hosts.
So buy a spooky costume,
And decorations too,
And I guarantee
That you and me
Will scare someone with
BOO!

My Dream Jack o Lantern

My dream jack o lantern
Is very short and round.
It has a big fat stem,
The perfect hem,
About two feet from the ground.

My dream jack o lantern,
Has two scary triangle eyes.
A big fat stem, the perfect hem,
Scary triangle eyes.

My dream jack o lantern,
Has an upside down triangle nose.
A big fat stem, the perfect hem,
Scary triangle eyes,
An upside down triangle nose.

My dream jack o lantern, has a scary squiggly mouth.
A big fat stem, the perfect hem,
Scary triangle eyes,
An upside down triangle nose, a scary squiggly mouth!

My dream jack o lantern,
Someone please carve my description out!

Autumn, a Fantastic Season

Colored trees, of autumn leaves,
And holidays, full of great fun,
There's Halloween,
And Thanksgiving,
But swimming pools,
There are none.
The season that we begin school,
Autumn's better than April Fools!
The time when the wind blows the leaves to the ground,
And during their stay there, they go
Crunch-crunch!
But by winter, there are none to be found.
The weather will start to be cold,
And the short sleeves will start to get old,
The sky's red, orange, yellow, and brown, what a sight!
But one day, they'll be gone,
They'll leave overnight.
And when you wake up,
You'll see white everywhere,
That's taken the place,
Of the red, orange, yellow and brown.

Pumpkins Waiting

In the black darkness,
Of Halloween,
Something orange is sitting on the ground.
The orange are the pumpkins,
Waiting,
Waiting for the ghosts,
They're waiting,
For the action,
Just waiting, still as the moon,
They wait for witches,
To cackle,
And ghosts to come and haunt,
For spiders to surprise,
And black cats to crawl,
For all the spooks,
To scare, and scare, and scare.
You'll see the pumpkins, the spots of orange,
In the black,
Waiting on the doorsteps,
This night of ghosts,
And spooks.

Dried-up Fall Leaf

Brown, so crumbly,
Goes 'Crackle' when you touch it,
Feels so dry and hard,
The color is like some twigs,
Sounds like a fire,
Crackling, falls apart.

A Rainy Thanksgiving

It's raining, it's raining,
On Thanksgiving Day,
So the visiting families,
Can't go out and play,
And the floats will be
Pitter-pattered on,
This very grateful day,
Oh, it's raining, it's
Raining,
Like the month before
May.

Winter

Chanukiahs lit,
Christmas trees covered with lights,
Snow, so sparkling,
Like a newly polished dish,
The air, so freezing,
Children out
In magic.

Nights and Lights
On Chanukah

1 little, 2 little, 3 little nighty-nights,
4 little, 5 little, 6 little nighty-nights,
7 little, 8 little, yes, 8 little nighty-nights,
8 little nights of Chanukah.

1 little, 2 little, 3 little candles,
4 little, 5 little, 6 little candles,
7 little, 8 little, 8 little (and 1 big candle) on the menorah,
9 candles on the menorah.

1 little, 2 little, 3 little presents,
4 little, 5 little, 6 little presents,
7 little, 8 little, (and maybe some big presents,)
From relatives for Chanukah.

1 little, 2 little, 3 little children,
4 little, 5 little, 6 little children,
7 little, 8 little, 9 little children,
10 little children,
Ripping open presents,
Singing, dancing and praying,
Some are playing – dreidel they're playing,
Eating latkes – no, not matzah,
It's all happening, happening,
Oh – on Chann-u-kaah!

The Holiday of Chanukah

Chanukah, an 8 day holiday,
Oh, what fun!
And even if it is snowing or raining,
It feels like sun.
Presents, presents, presents galore,
But dreidels, dreidels, every year we get more.
We eat our gelt, as we watch candle one melt.
Oh, oh, oh, what a sad sight,
1 day gone, 7 more nights.

Winter

Glistening wonders,
Falling, for children to play,
Freezing, though dazzling,
Sparkling, like great magic,
Beautiful while there,
Crunching, crisp, and cold,
Fun for many games,
Glistening in the sky.

Snow

White little flakes, falling from the sky,
So fun to play in,
O-oh me-oh-my!
These frozen drops of rain,
All look the same,
But each one is different in so many ways.
It's a snow day! A snowy-snowy day!
Let's go out and play!
Hip-hip-hooray!
Snowy snowy day! Yay yay yay!
Snowy-snowy day.
Snowy snow day!

Wintertime, a Joyful Time

Wintertime, a joyful time, full of
snow and other magical things.
Wintertime, a magical time
What surprises will this winter
bring?
What surprises will it bring?

Passover Night with my Family

Passover night, a night full of fun,
Kids, parents, everyone!
Families all throughout the street,
Singing Pesach songs as they eat!

Children answer the four questions,
Search for the afikomen,
I can't wait until Passover comes again!

Matzah

On Pesach we can't have regular bread,
So matzah's what we eat instead!
Flat and crispy, this bread is, yes,
And it's God who helped us get it,
He we bless.

Flat and crispy, with butter it's better,
Better than a brand new sweater,
Matzah is a treat, I must say,
'Specially on Passover day.

The Afikomen

Dad breaks the middle matzah in half,
We close our eyes, try to peek, then start to laugh,
Dad's hiding it for us to try and find,
Is it over something, under something or behind?
I can't wait till Passover day, for this is a game you don't always
Get to play!

The Story of Passover

Long ago in Egypt, we used to be slaves,
But God said to Moses, "Go to Pharoah,"
So he did, he was so brave.
When Moses asked Pharoah to let his
People go, Pharoah's answer was no, no, no.
God sent nine plagues but Pharoah still said no,
But that last one convinced him to let the Jewish people go.
But while the Jewish people got close to Israel, yes,
Pharoah changed his mind, God spread the Red Sea open only for us, so He we bless.
We sing Dayanu to say it would have
Been enough, it would,
We sing it to say "Thank you"
Like good people should.

Love

Love is sweet, sweetness is kindness, kindness is caring and caring is happiness!
Happiness is joyful, joy is glory,
And glory is the earth.
The earth is beauty, and beauty is peace, and peace
Is love.

Rain

Pitter, patter, splash,
Like a blanket of water,
Drip, drop, drip drip drop.

Summer

Swimming and playing,
The warm sun's like a fun holder,
Laughing all day long.

Music
Written with Kyra

Music, something I can hear,
Ringing, ringing, in my ear,
Music fills me up with pride,
Like staring at a beautiful bride.

Music comes in many kinds,
Percussion, brass, strings and woodwinds,
Then of course there is singing and humming,
Which make a beautiful sound with plucking or drumming.

So listen to a musical note,
Pay attention to how it's wrote,
Maybe someday you'll write a great song,
But remember to always sing along.

Evergreen Leaf

Feels like summer grass,
Rubbing against my bare feet,
Smells like a pine cone,
A smell that is so unique,
Looks scratchy, leaf green,
Like that for all seasons.

Peace
Written with Christy Dwyer

Peace is love,
peace is kind and caring.
Peace is happiness and sharing!
Peace can be music or silence, but
peace is not violence.

Haikus

Warm, cozy fire,
Sitting here it's oh-so-warm,
A wonderful place.

Dark, cold, rainy day,
Like a miserable, fierce night,
Pit-pat on the roof.

Good home once again,
Glad to be out of the rain,
Simple, but nice home.

Where?

In the cold black night,
I see a sight,
I see a light.
I think to myself,
"What's it doing out there?"
Then it makes a strange sort of look,
Out in the cold air,
Then I can tell that this is one of a kind,
No pair.
All alone out there.
But there is where?
Where is there?
Where is there?
Where. . .

The Sensational Strawberry Festival
A Poem about the Environment-themed Strawberry Festival!

A raffle, a moon bounce, a cakewalk, some rides,
Lots of games and cool prizes, and a few awesome slides!
Eat strawberries and ice cream; make some colorful art with sand,
There's also a wax-candle making stand.

Win a pizza party by selling tickets for ice cream,
Buy T-shirts supporting the world being green,
Help save the planet using the "blue bin,"
There are so many prizes to earn and to win!

Strawberry Festival will be a blast this year,
Everyone will be joyful; we'll all scream and cheer,
So come to raise money and have lots of fun,
It's one of the reasons our school's number 1!

The Hamptons

Grass, green as a frog,
Sky, blue as the ocean waves,
Flowers, as colorful as rainbows,
Hedges for all that I can see.

Sad

Lonely, Bored,
Crying, Falling, Hurting,
Frown, Tear, Smile, Leap,
Skipping, Cheering, Playing,
Games, Fun,
Happy

All Kinds of Families
Written with Christy Dwyer and Lydia Bier

All kinds of families, big and small, they have many different traditions,
Even different religions!
Brothers, sisters, uncles, aunts, cousins, too,
I am part of a family and so are you!
Mothers, fathers, grandparents, more!
Relatives all over, families galore!

My Emotions

I smell the smell of a laundry room,
On a cold, winter day,
The best smell on Earth.

I hear the sound of a lullaby,
The best sound on Earth.

I taste the taste of cookie cake,
The best taste on Earth.

I feel the feel of a Zingo card,
The best feel on Earth.

I see the sight of nature and peace,
The best sight on Earth.

Holidays

Holidays, fun and games,
And many beautiful sights,
Time for shows,
And lights that glow,
Lots of food, and late-staying-up nights.
But the best part of the season,
Is one special reason,
No matter what games you play,
No matter the holidays,
No matter the food,
It's being with your families
Each day.

Reading

Magical, Exciting,
Traveling, Learning, Wondering,
Stories, Characters, Plans, Creations,
Brainstorming, Thinking, Imagining,
Invent, Create,
Writing

Ocean

Wet, salty,
Waving, splashing, crashing,
Fish-filled, coral land,
Towers, beaches,
Blowing, building, digging,
Grainy, dry,
Sand

Orange

Orange is like the sound of crunching leaves blowing in Autumn wind.
Orange is like the smell of Halloween with pumpkins' scents filling streets.
Orange is like the taste of a juicy orange fruit's goodness coming to your lips.
Orange is like the feel of the warm sun, a promising start to a summer's day.

Trees

Leafy, strong
Blowing, rustling, growing,
Trees help us breathe
Plants

Leaf

Crisp,
Colorful,
Crunching,
Rakers cause
Bunching,
Piles soon
Will form,
In the children storm.

Friendship is . . .

Friendship is a sun, all of the rays are friends.

Friendship is a cake, and all of the ingredients are unique friends.

Friendship is a field and all of the plants are friends.

Suns, cakes and fields are like friendship – the big, final result would not be possible if
it was not made up of friends who care about each other.

My Birthday

It's my birthday, hooray, hooray!
(This doesn't happen every day!)
So I'll dance, sing and play, because today's my birthday!

Everyone's comin' for a party,
So far, nobody is tardy,
Boy, this day is great!
And oh, the cake, I can't wait!

My birthday was a blast!
But it went by oh-so-fast,
Tomorrow's the party in school,
At least that will make my birthday end in a way that's cool, that'll rule.

Storms

Whirling, whirling wind,
Little raindrops falling down.
Pitter, patter, splash!
Thunder booms, full of terror,
Lightning streaks the sky,
I wish the sun would
Come.

Helping

Kind, generous,
Caring, giving, encouraging,
Volunteer, shelter, party, criminal,
Bragging, bossing, keeping,
Selfish, lazy,
Neglecting

Reading

Reading is a mountain, stuck on rocks of suspense, and once you get down you can climb up again.

Reading is a key – to get to new worlds, the library is where tickets are sold.

Reading is a planet, and books are the rockets you use to go up to outer space and explore.

I am from . . .

I am from selling lemonade on a day like a turned on stove.

I am from singing prayers and learning them from the rabbi in temple.

I am from learning twirls and leaps in ballet and then showing them in the recitals.

I am from getting the notes right in piano, then playing a wonderful song.

I am from having fun playing and creating things with friends, something everyone enjoys.

I am from reading for long stretches of time, when there's nothing I would rather do.

I am from eating some of the few foods I enjoy, pasta, chicken nuggets, and chocolate.

I am from fun vacations, so many different experiences of a good time.

I am from running 3 miles around Taylor Park, a great yet sweaty goal to achieve.

I am from fighting with my sister Kyra, although we always work out our reasons in the end.

I am from writing stories, some true, some not, and some I will treasure forever.

I am from being these things for my whole life, along with more, and the events of the future.

Helping is. . .

Helping is a study, in school all who take it learn to do good deeds.

Helping is a gift, given to special people that are told to pass it on.

Helping is the future, when we help, we can make the world of our children scintillate.

Millburn

Millburn makes me think of friendship,
Together all the time,
Millburn makes me think of neighbors,
With a house by mine.
Millburn makes me think of schools,
Some of the best five,
Reading, writing, math and more,
Keeps our brains alive.
Millburn makes me think of changes,
Going on and on,
1-5-0 years of fun,
Improvements have come,
And bad things have gone.
So Millburn makes me think of days,
The old and the new,
The fun we'll share will always be there,
Millburn, we love you!

Shabbat B'Shir Poem
Written with Carly Mazer

The band booms,
The prayers ring,
Spirited people cheer
and sing.

Little kids enjoy themselves,
Grownups have fun too,
The doors of prayer
all open up,
We hope you will come through.

The rabbis are all awesome,
They lead us in our prayer,
Afterwards there's always yummy food
to eat and to share.

The Cantor is so cheerful,
with him we all will sing,
Celebrating Shabbat
is a really cool thing!

Flying

Flying is a sport; your score is high when you have gotten the goal of maneuvering a plane.

Flying is an adventure, an airplane is your tour guide to lead you through the
excitement of the sky.

Flying is a dance, the stage is the air and the aircraft does the routine.

Super bowl

It's Super bowl 2008,
February 3rd is the honored date!

The Giants, who will win, in red or in blue
Step onto the field where the Patriots boo.

Neither New York nor New England will host,
An Arizona stadium is the chosen place to boast.

People all over will watch the big game,
Which will be the team to win glory and fame?

A Rainy Day
Written with Carly Mazer and Brittany Strear

Raindrops dance and raindrops play,
On this dark and dreary day,
The clouds will cry, the sun won't stay,
On this bleak and light less day.

The plants reach out to get their share,
Water glistens everywhere.
To only ducks this day is fair,
This humid day with moistened air!

Raindrops drum and raindrops soar,
Everything seems like a bore.
There are many umbrellas and puddles galore,
It's as if dryness and clear skies would exist no more.

Springtime

Cheer is in the air,
Beautiful flowers grow tall,
Birds fly over trees,
A crisp feeling of beauty,
Animals creep out,
Amazing time of year.

Beautiful time, children playing,
Sports can be played,
Wondrous feelings fill the air,
Amazing things underground,
In the sky.

Rain

Dancing on the slippery ground,
Making people rush,
In the summer, a great relief,
In winter, it turns snow to mush.

Wet and cold, streaming down from the sky,
Like it has a leak,
Crayons coloring the sky gray,
On the window it leaves a clear streak.

Like candy coming from the piñata clouds
A machine turning dirt into mud,
Leaving trees heavy with raindrops,
Magic that helps flowers bud.

Clouds

Floating through the sky,
Up, to wondrous places,
Big, fluffy pillows.
They go up to the heavens,
Slept on by angels.
Pushed by the blowing
Wind.

Inspiring Places

Jerusalem

People strolling, rising up,
Cafés all start to bake,
Heading off, out for the day,
Jerusalem awakes.

Seeing sights, exploring round,
Gathering to pray,
All are bustling about,
Jerusalem, by day.

Pink clouds blow in above the peaks,
The moon is not here yet,
The orange sky behind the walls,
Jerusalem, at sunset.

All is lit up, the sky is dark,
There is no need to fight,
So calm and peaceful,
Spectacular too,
Jerusalem, at night.

Wyoming

A beautiful sight wherever you turn,
Wyoming.
Ranches, rivers, lakes, waterfalls,
Wyoming.
Elk and bison grazing out in fields
Wyoming.
Cloudless skies over all kinds of mountains
Wyoming.
A bird faintly chirps from one of the thousands of trees
Wyoming.
Bushes, wildflowers and creeks cover the mountains,
Wyoming.
Glorious, natural sights of national parks,
Wyoming.

On Wyoming's Mountains

On the mountains of Wyoming,
There are many things to see,
Some big, some small, some short, some tall,
What a wonder to me!
First I pass the patches of bright colored wildflowers,
Their petals blow, they dance, so slow,
It's Mother Nature's power.
Cover the whole mountain,
There are bushes and trees,
Such a sight is this green!
How noble, like a queen!
All blowing in the breeze.
A dried up stream is curving,
Down and down it winds,
It's now all stones, so hard like bones,
Filled with water only in my mind.
A bird is faintly chirping,
Great falls come rushing down,
And in the night, oh what a sight!
With the wildlife out, you won't frown.
Underneath the mountain,
There's even more to see,
Fun things to do, and more great views,
To a fun trip, Wyoming's the key.

Creepy Cats

Sly cats, creeping,
Quietly sneaking,
Mysteriously appearing,
Slinking round,
Throughout the town,
In the dark, a cat leaps –
I am tearing!

Jumping up in windows,
Darting under things,
Creeping out at night,
Meowing – the cat sings!
Spirits of the dead,
Looking for their friends,
I think that one's my grandpa,
The cats – they never end!

Rooftop Questions

Looking down at the Wall,
Swarming with people,
A large crowd of black,
A small one of skirts,
Why is the men's side so much bigger?

Dancing the hora to niguns,
"Li, li, li,"
A circle of men, and a circle of women,
Why don't the girls dance with the men here?

Staring towards the Dome of the Rock,
A gold, round top,
A colorful base,
A holy location, first ours, now the Muslims,
Why won't they let us in there?

Heading down to pray at the Wall,
Why is everyone dressed that way?
Why does everyone cry?
Why do they walk backwards?

Coming back up,
For more Kabbalat Shabbat,
You can hear the prayer back at the Wall,
And the call of the Arabs, it's their Shabbat too,
Arabs and Jews are so similar –
Why can't we just get along?

Staring down at the glorious view,
Lights come on every building,
Thinking about the spectacular city,
Thanking God for bringing us here.

Havdalah Night

Anxiously peering out the window,
Waiting for the dark to come,
"Can we do Havdalah yet?"
When the light drains from the sky,
And the moon takes the sun's place,
We head up to the rooftop
For Havdalah.
When we arrive we are singing, holding the blue and white braided candle,
Lighting it, keeping it alive.
Then, arms around each other, we sing the prayer for the spices,
Smelling them as they are passed along the circle.
Finally, the Kiddush, we say our prayer for the wine.
The rabbi sips it out of the silver cup,
And Shabbat is over,
We have made Havdalah.
"Shavuah tov" to all,
Have a good week!
We end with a song,
Dancing the hora by moonlight.
All week long we anticipate Shabbat,
All Shabbat long we ask, "Can we do Havdalah yet?"

Wonders of the Wall

Tears fall onto limestone,
Tears of remembrance,
Remembrance of tragedy.
Prayer books clutched in hands, pressed on hearts.
Fingers touch the stone,
Stones of memories,
Memories of destruction.
Stepping away in awe and honor,
Honor of this wonderful sight.
Beggars holding cups of *shekels*,
Each coin is so small to us but means the world to them.
People insert slips of paper
In this mailbox, a mailbox full of
Notes and prayers to be delivered
To God.
Joy, sadness, holiness, and solemness fill the air,
The air around the Western Wall.

A Dazzling First Day Discovery

Early in the morning,
Groggy and tired from a seven and a half hour night of sleep,
But too restless to make it nine,
I creep out of my bed and my room in the hotel,
Which seems rather ordinary from my view of it at 11 o'clock last night,
Except for the cacti lining the driveway.
My mother and sister, up already, say,
"Come, you'll like this."
So I follow and discover an exquisite Arizona backyard!

A little round cactus, small and alone, sits in front of me,
What is he thinking? Is he crying? Does he want to be my friend?
Is he too shy to come close? Are all the other cacti mean to him?
Nearby, a flower bush stands a little bit away from the plant party,
Is she older and wiser, is she watching over this little Lone One?

Then, all together, a crowd of cacti! A celebration!
Big ones with massive balloon-shaped leaves, full of spikes,
Going every which way! Many of them, scattered in the cacti garden.
There are bushes of cacti, with long arms reaching out – to strangle or to help? I'm not
sure!

Then, way back, beyond countless kinds of cacti,
Dried up streams with only stones in them,
Trees standing tall with bird nests perched on top, is a proud, majestic cactus,
Senor Saguaro,
With strong arms and a straight body,
Watching over his kingdom – the magical garden of cacti.

Sky View of Arizona

Mountains, dotted with trees, pointing up to the sky,
Small lines run through, they may be dried creeks or roads.
Behind these mountains, there are plateaus, flat-topped green tables,
Carved into shapes by God's hands.
Then, behind the layer of plateaus, more mountains!
It's a mountain-plateau-mountain sandwich!

The plane keeps flying and the scenery changes,
Soon, we are over formations of red rock, all different unique, freeform creations,
Made of the rusty rock – and not just random shapes, mountains of it too!
Whole mountains of red! Tall hills, the color of bricks, with white streaked lines
Etching through, with green mountaintops too.
Red cliffs are also in view, with cracks in the cliffs,
So many formations in this unique sculpture garden of red rock!

The plane keeps flying, and we see snow!
Snow on the mountains in Flagstaff!
Just minutes ago, we'd been over barren deserts! Now we were seeing snow!
The change of scene is just a sample of our small world,
In only miles, everything can change.
Each part of the flight, each part of the world
Is unique.

Finally, we fly over our destination – the Grand Canyon!
Layers leading down to the deep hole,
Orange and red lined layers,
Cliffs branching off,
Steep inclines going down,
Plateaus cover the top,
Layers and layers, all uniquely colored and shaped,
Leading down about a mile to the massive hole.
All these layers, they are like people,
The top layer is what everyone sees,
And each deeper layer shows something closer to your true feelings and beliefs,
All leading up to the Grand Canyon in each of us,
That shows what we are really made of.

Optimism

I'm like water, wiggling, jiggling,
I'm like water, but I can never spill!

The pilot told us that the air is like water; it splashes around a little,
That is why this plane is bumping in the air, shaking me,
I think I left my stomach a little higher up; I'm twisting to the side in my seat,
But I think optimistically, and tell myself:
I'm like water, wiggling, jiggling,
I'm like water, but I can never spill!

This half full cup of water will never spill!
This optimistic person won't even need that plastic bag!
If everyone in the world thought they were half full,
And would never spill, or break, or fall,
Then they could have a certain power over themselves, and could change themselves
And the world for the positive – with optimism!

Hidden Treasure

The water sprays and rises up
And bends and curves and stretches
The sways, in perfect coordination with each other,
In rhythmic harmony with the music,
How does something so still and boring,
So plain
Such an everyday usual necessity
Create a treasure
A dazzling choreography
Who knew?

And the beautiful dancing is surrounded
By ancient architecture
And faraway monuments
Imitated all in one street
Such spectacular wonders,
And cars rush by on the street,
As if nothing is there to look at
These buildings are beautiful gemstones
In a jewelry box that is hidden
Amongst the ordinary,
Who knew that a treasure could be inside?

Those who look know.
Those who stop to see know.
Those who can take a moment out of the hustle and bustle and ordinary business can
see the true treasure of life.
They can see that something ordinary can easily bend and curve and stretch and
become a graceful dancer.
So take a minute to stop and discover and look,
To find the choreography, the jewel
Hidden away in the treasure box of everyday.
Then you will know that there can be a sparkle amongst the dull,
That beauty can be found anywhere and anything can transform to be a wonder,
If you just look hard enough.

People I Love

The Skills of my Sister

Splash! With a graceful dive, she enters the pool, swiftly swimming across,
Strong, she is, keeping up her rapidness lap after lap,
That mermaid, the one skillfully and marvelously maintaining this hasty pace,
Never running out of energy as she swims,
She is my sister – such an agile, magnificent, powerful, speedy figure,
Amazing how well she can swim in the pool.
Determined to practice too, forever eager to practice no matter how early she must
wake up, or what activities she may miss, she is always ready and enthusiastic to
practice so she can improve, even though she is so talented all ready.

Did you hear that her artwork is being taken to the Ed Center?
Only a few children from each grade will have this honor.
She is one, it is not surprising that she is, and she definitely deserves it,
For she can draw pictures that look like the real object,
And when she colors in every last detail, so caringly, absorbed and always concentrating
on the superb work she is doing,
It makes her artwork come to life.
This gifted artist is my sister, who has a fantastic drawing talent and deserves this
reward for her creative and unbelievable work.

She's the most intelligent girl in her class, I believe,
She can add numbers with three or four digits, and does it quite quickly,
And almost always gets the answer right.
When she sets her mind to it, this girl would never tire of adding numbers, she is so
dedicated to learning.
She could read books that some children in fourth or fifth grade would struggle with!
If you were to look on her refrigerator, you would see the incredible amount of spelling
tests on which she got a perfect score!
This brilliant girl is my sister – quick and correct with numbers, extremely advanced in
reading, always right in spelling, and dedicated to learning too.

Crack! Do you know how far she can hit a baseball?
Over the fence! Home run!
It's so solid, it's so fierce,
Get out of the way if it's coming – it will knock you over!
And she dribbles the ball . . . and she shoots, and SCORES!
In basketball, she is a star dribbler and she can score too!
She speeds across the field in her soccer games, kicking the ball, passing the ball,
shooting and scoring!
She's also a dancer, so poised and stylish in all her positions,
And this #1, super-hard hitter, this able, gifted basketball player, this strong soccer star,
This dazzling dancer,
She's my sister too!

So kind, always having great ideas to help others,
Cares so much about the environment, about animals, about less fortunate people,
It's extraordinary how thoughtful she is, especially at such a young age,
And she has such a talent to make people laugh,
Her grin is contagious!
Everyone loves to be around her, I know it,
Only a fool would not praise or admire her,
With every year, this girl earns more charm,
And now she's turning eight!
This too-remarkable-for-words swimmer, this artistic, brainy girl, this athlete, this dancer, this kind and enjoyable, humorous person, is also my sister, and even though sometimes I don't show it,
I love her, for her numerous talents and qualities that everyone knows, and also for one more – the trait of being the best sister anyone could ever have.

To Kyra –
The Talents of a Good Sister

Sports and reading, music and art,
You're good at so many things 'cause you're so smart,
Basketball, tennis, having some fun,
If I had 10 sisters, you'd be #1.

You're cool and you're funny, clever and kind,
The best sister ever with a needle sharp mind,
You beat me in games, of cards and of sports,
You're talented, bold, and kind,
A quite special sort.

Good at so many things, having such a blast,
Being so friendly, bright and so fast,
The one thing only one special person could do,
Is be the best sister, 'cause that is just YOU.

You are the Greatest
A Poem about Rabbi Debbie Bravo

You are the greatest, one of the best people I've met,
You're one of the smartest, one of the best kinds yet.
I like how you clap, to a great rhythm, an exciting beat,
It makes everybody get up and sing on their feet.
The way that you pray is so wonderful,
the best,
It is so special, different from all
the rest.

You're someone I admire, you're a
role model for me,
You're an amazing person, really
someone I'd like to be.
So even though I'll miss you, 'cause you won't be here to see,
The place that you're going to is
Really lucky!

I Love You Daddy!

Daddy, you are a counselor, encouraging me to experience adventure and do things that I might be a little scared of. Daddy, without you, I would never have had the joy and excitement of bike-riding or the relaxing and pleasing experience of swimming in the ocean. Without you, I wouldn't play softball, and I wouldn't have ever entered the world of Harry Potter. Even if I had decided to read Harry Potter, or play softball, or ride a bike, or go in the ocean one day without your encouragement, it wouldn't have been for a very long time, and it wouldn't be the same without you there, coaching me, riding with me, swimming with me, or reading to me. Sometimes, you give me a little extra push to do something, and I may not want you to at the time, but later I will be grateful that you nag me to do something I fear. You give me that little push, something only you can give to me. I may get mad when you tell me to do something I don't want to do, but now I realize I am so lucky to have you – an encouraging counselor, a little extra push that I don't always want, but really do need, to get me to do new things. You expand my limits from somewhere a little above the ground to the sky. There are some things only a dad can give a daughter – certain encouragement, a little extra push, and one more thing – a special type of love that dads give daughters, and that daughters get from no one else but dads. You've given me all of this, and I know you will continue to give me all of this for a very, very long time. And Daddy, I know not everyone is lucky enough to have someone like you. Thank you for being so great. There are so many joys in life that I never would have experienced without you. I love you so much, Daddy!

Fabulous Fathers

Fathers are entertaining; they'll always make you grin,
Whether playing sports or a family board game, they'll teach you how to win.

Fathers are encouraging; they motivate you to do your best,
In anything, fathers accomplish so much – let's give our dads some rest.

Fathers are so cozy; it's always nice to cuddle and hug,
Huddling up in bed together, it's pleasing to feel so snug.

Fathers are so intelligent; they'll try to pass this to us,
So on this day to honor dads and all they do, let's not give them a fuss.

Fathers are so diligent; doing hard work everyday,
So instead of pestering our awesome dads, let's respect them extra on Father's Day.

Happy Birthday!
I Love You!

Grandma Harriet, affectionate and sweet,
Spending lots of time with you is quite a special treat,
Grandma Harriet, caring and cheerful too,
I love when I will call you and we discuss all that we do.

Grandma Harriet, the times we have are grand,
When you sleep over at my house, our fun's a unique brand,
Grandma Harriet, hugging me all the time,
So generous and helpful, I'm happy that you're mine.

Grandma Harriet, always acting kind,
You're a special person - a type sometimes difficult to find,
Grandma Harriet, you constantly make me smile,
If you took a "loving grandma" test, then you would pass the trial.

Grandma Harriet, everyday you love me,
And this week, you just had a birthday, now you're 70,
So now that you're a brand new age, I have something to say,
I love you because you're sweet, fun, and so kind,
And you love me everyday.

Grandmas are . . .

Grandmas are candy; it is a delicious treat to spend time with them.

Grandmas are bandages, when the troubles of life scrape the grandchildren's knees,
the sweetness and love of grandmas can heal the wounds of the world's problems.

Grandmas are blankets, they are always there to keep you warm and be a protecting
shield over you. They make you feel cozy and protected.

Grandmas are diaries, you can tell them all about life, all your troubles, victories
and irritations, and they will always listen to your stories without complaining or
interrupting.

Super Grandma Toby!

Grandma Toby
A grandma so fine
With 3 grandchildren
Each one unique and divine.

Courtney, Kyra and Asher
With her whole heart she loves them all
They are all so different,
So she does different things to show she cares,
So many diverse acts of love – some very big, and some small.

For Courtney, the oldest, she'll take her to dinner or a play,
Give her chocolate and drive her where she needs,
A hug or a phone call is always in store,
And of course, she'll listen to the poems she writes and reads.

Kyra, the middle grandchild, is so busy,
So of course Grandma drives her some places too,
She'll watch a sport game or a swim meet of hers,
Play a game, take her to a show or out for food.

Courtney and Kyra also love to sleep over,
To play card games, to swim in the pool,
Grandma's door is always open for them to come on in
As long as they don't steal her shoes – that game is cruel!

And finally the youngest – Asher,
Although he's only a year old,
Whenever he sees Grandma,
His smile is bright and bold.

Even though Asher lives farther away,
And Grandma can't see him very much,
Grandma shows she cares about him by Skyping
So they can always keep in touch.

Of course Grandma's always happy,
To play Peek-a-Boo, read a book or play with a toy,
Who knows how much fun Grandma will have with Asher
When he grows up to be a big boy!

So Grandma loves her grandchildren
They are all special in different ways
And no matter what she's doing with them
Her love for her grandchildren forever stays.

Little Baby Miracles

Miracles can be three-month-early twin babies that have to stay in the hospital for a month and have numerous operations. The babies are tiny, but those little miracles survive.

Miracles can sleep until 10:30 in the morning on a hot summer day. They can pull themselves up and stare at their sister, still sleeping in the crib beside her. They can jump up and down and smile and cry when their mother and their two new older friends go to carry their twin downstairs. They can laugh and jump and sit while one of their friends decides to stay with them.

Miracles can be carried downstairs. They can copy older kids, bang on small pianos, crawl all over, walk a few steps. They can eat Cheerios and put a few down their shirt. They can climb on you, strap your shoes, pull your glasses, and touch your nose. Little baby miracles are always curious, and always happy.

Miracles, especially the little baby ones, can move us. They can make us realize how much good and luck and wonder and happiness there actually is in this world. They can cry when you leave them, but next time we see them again, they'll laugh and climb on us and copy us again. Little baby miracles like these can always make us happy, especially when they are adorable twins named Chloe and Isabelle.

I Love You, Pop!
April 2009

Pop, you are so generous; you give so much to everyone,
To me, it's raisinettes and gifts and love and outings full of fun,
To others, it's money for those in need or wise words in a speech,
People everywhere come to hear you talk; you must have lots to teach.

Pop, you are so loving; you always care so much about me,
You take me lots of places, like to plays I want to see,
You devote some time to listen to how I'm doing, to hear all about what's new in school,
And in the summer days – for me – you'll heat and let me swim in your pool!

Pop, have a happy birthday, enjoy your special day,
You deserve to take a break and have a great time today!
And if for some reason, you are ever feeling down or blue,
Read this poem over again so you'll be reminded of all the reasons that I love you!

Happy Birthday, Pop!

Pop, on your birthday,
We should celebrate,
To reward you for all that
You give and donate.

Pop, on your birthday,
We should honor you
And recognize all the hard work
That you do.

Pop, on your birthday,
You deserve to have fun;
A reward for all of the
Good things you have done.

Pop, on your birthday,
I think we all agree,
You should get a big hug for
The love you've given me.

The Many Sides of Pop

Pop, an amazing grandpa,
Always caring about me,
He gives me Raisinettes and hugs
This is the Leon Cooperman that I most often see.

But there's also businessman Pop
A successful, hardworking guy,
Fairly famous – he's been in the news and on TV,
For the stocks he sells and buys.

Then there's the Pop who gives so much money
The philanthropist that supports worthy organizations,
A kind, charitable man who helps and donates so much,
Traits worthy of being passed down the generations!

There are so many causes that Pop has helped,
And the family foundation was started by Pop,
I'm so excited to be a part of it,
To make good programs start and bad things in the world stop.

Hence, Pop is a really cool grandpa,
A famous, prosperous businessman too,
A charitable person who started a great family foundation,
What else could someone possibly do?

So when I go out somewhere with Pop,
I always feel full of pride,
That this prominent man that I'm with is my grandpa,
This loving person here at my side.

Dear Mommy

It's finally the special day of the year when the spotlight points to moms, the people who cook and care and love and no matter what, they can stay calm! They do so much for their children's lives, without moms, where would we be? And what recognition do they ever get? Well, you're a lucky mom – you've got this letter from me!

Thanks for understanding me, and hearing about what's going on in my life, and thanks for always protecting me, so I never experience strife. You make me all my food, you respect my interests and thoughts, there's a whole long list of things you do for me, ever since I was a tot. But you're a mom and it's Mother's Day, so today you'll take a break, from doing all the work you do and making all you make. Today, I'll take some of the jobs off your hand and I'll do them by myself, of course, someone else might give me a hand, but you can relax – you don't need to help!

Your wish is my command today, what you want, from me you'll get! If you're uncomfortable or not at ease, I'm on the way, don't fret! A massage, breakfast, a bubble bath, a concert, I'll do whatever you say! After all, you do so much all the time, but you get a break on Mother's Day!

Your loving daughter,
Courtney

Mommy Motivating Me to Do Mitzvot
A poem that appreciates and recognizes all you do for the world and me

Mommy, you are a trail in a forest of wrong turns, you will teach me how to get through tough times in the world and how to do righteous acts. You inform me what some problems there are in life today, you tell me what incorrect ways to go there are in these woods. You notify me how I can bring others on this path of answers to challenging problems in life; you guide me on the journey of goodness and thoughtful deeds. You are a role model to me, you make me joyful to witness you bringing happiness to others, and I am also cheerful when I can bring pleasure to the less fortunate myself. Yet I would be nowhere without your words and acts, for you are the inspiration that gives me the advice and examples I need to do these mitzvot. You also help me carry out my ideas I have to help the world. You are the one that gives me all I require to accomplish these moral acts of giving to those who could use a spirit booster. I look up to you, all the actions you take are seen by me and they are all admired too. Projects and events you work so hard on inspire me to go out in the world and do some of my own, but without your actions, support, teachings, and help, I probably wouldn't be able to go on with mitzvot that I love and always try to do. You always give affection to me and I try my best to pass your kindness on to others, and maybe one day compassion will touch everyone in the world all the time. If this happens, then everyone will thank the people like you who work so hard everyday making the world a better place and inspiring their daughters to do so too.

Generation to Generation

Up there
I see you
Hundreds of eyes staring at you
I don't know what the words all mean
But I think I know what you're talking about

The gold shimmers
I clutch the star
Yes – I don't know what the words all mean
But I definitely know what you're talking about

That star – it was passed to you
You passed to me six years ago
And I will pass it on

More than a piece of jewelry was passed
Love was passed
And even more

One day
I hope that you will see me
Up there
Hundreds of eyes staring at me
And you'll probably know what the words all mean
But you'll really feel what I'm talking about

The necklace is a symbol
More than just a star
Yes, it stands for Judaism
Yes, it will always remind me of my heritage
My traditions
My people
My past
My religion

It will also remind me of more
It will remind me of values – not as a Jew, but as a person
Values that must be passed from generation to generation
Or else they will not travel anymore

Thank you for passing down the necklace, Mommy
You've also passed down values and tradition
So I don't remember much about that speech
Except generation to generation
And holding the necklace in my hand
And knowing that I've got a job to do ahead of me

Spit

The cards
Sliding in your hand
One by one
The cards come

We set up
One up, four down
One up, three down,
One up, two down
One up, one down
One up

Spit!
The game has begun

The sound of the cards
Slap, floosh, flap
Flipping
Slapping
Landing on piles
Until one has no more

Then we pick our teams
Our pile of soldiers
With only our eyes – no more
And sometimes we don't know
We guess
And sometimes we are right
And sometimes not

And the process repeats
One up, four down
One up, three down,
One up, two down
One up, one down
One up

Spit!

The sound of the cards landing on piles
Picking our teams with only our eyes
Until one has no more
And the champion is declared

And I just love the way I can say, "Rematch?"
And we both know just what game

A Birthday Poem to Jodi

A ring will glisten,
A bracelet will glow.
But you'll shine much more than those,
I know.
A necklace will look good,
Earrings will impress,
But something looks better,
I must confess:

Your ear to ear smile is bound to amaze,
The great way you act will leave most in a daze
And how you do so much in so little time,
Cannot be expressed in a poem or a rhyme.

You are so incredible in every which way,
That's why there's an extra....
Happy Birthday!

Mommy, My Role Model

A role model is someone who has made choices in their life that benefit others. They do not only care about themselves; they know that they are part of a bigger picture. Therefore they work to paint it beautifully.

A role model is someone who is persistent. They will jump over hurdles and push past obstacles to win the race. A role model is strong. A role model never gives up.

A role model can be someone famous, but most often those "role models" are really just talented, famous, glamorous people. They are not really role models. Role models may just be matches. Yet they cause a great fire for those they are role models to. Role models may only do something small, but they inspire and influence people so greatly. Then maybe those people will become role models for others, and they will continue to pass on the spark and the fire will continue to burn even stronger.

Role models directly affect lives. They inspire and influence how others will live, or what they will grow up to be. Role models create role models. One person who is shaped by a role model may stimulate another. Who knows? Maybe role models have role models too.

Mommy, you are a role model. You work so hard to help others. You never give up. You face challenges. You have definitely started a spark in me that will continually make a difference in the world. In the big picture of things, maybe all the work you do is small, but without you, the big picture would never be painted beautifully. You directly affect my life. You say that I'm a role model to you, but I would only be part of who I am today without you. So really, I'm a role model because you are.

You stimulate me to do so many things, but I do them myself. You unlocked the doors, but I try to open them myself. A role model does not live someone's life for them, but merely points them in the right direction, and the direction you point me and will continue to point me in is one that I know will lead me to great places. A mother like you is someone special –a role model, that gets a daughter started on doing great things, and helps them on the way. Thank you for lighting my fire and continuing to supply the fuel that makes the flame burn.

Special Celebration

You're two of the most special people,
Both of you are one-of-a-kind,
Each of you is unique, I love you so much,
You're a special type of person that's not easy to find.

Mommy, everyone who sees you will fall in love with your kind smile,
Like Daddy did on this date a few years back,
And Daddy, your sense of humor and incredibly sharp mind,
Have made it so everyone is full of admiration for you,
Surely no one has a lack.

Two special, great people like you deserve
To stop and take a break,
From working so hard and doing so much
And making all you make.
And look what day it is today –
It's your anniversary!
So have a fun day with each other,
Celebrate with cheer and glee!

Two special people together,
So funny, so smart, so kind,
Celebrating a happy anniversary,
That's very hard to find.

Grandma Sylvia

To Grandma Sylvia, who will never hear this poem on Earth, but she will hear it in a happy place where she is healthy, for in her last years on Earth she was dying, but up in Heaven she is alive.

I had never seen a dead person
Unless you count under a grave
But I had never stared into a dead person's eyes
I had never touched a dead person
Sure, I'd touched graves,
But I had never touched the coldness of a dead person's skin
I had seen a dying person
A struggling person
In a hospital bed
Machines attached to her
Nurses around her
She'd made it so far
Would she die in that bed?
Would she make it back home?
She'd been sick in the hospital for days, maybe a week, before we came,
At first my sister and I didn't know
Then they told us
Some people said we shouldn't go
We shouldn't remember her like that
But we should see her, for it may have been the last chance
And we would cheer her up
And we went
And we did
I had touched a dying person
Given her a card
Sung to her
Held her hand
Looked into her eyes
I saw longing
A calm, yet restless spirit,
Wanting to fight through, wanting to let go,
Seeing us made a machine beep
Mommy said it wasn't bad
It meant she was excited
We made it beep! We made it beep!
We made her happy
Maybe that's why she fought and held on so long
All those years, and those last few days
She held on for 4 or 5 days after we saw her
And then she let go

She looked peaceful in that bed
She never made it back home
But if happiness was home, then she made it
I know she's happy in the sky
In Heaven
And I'll remember her not as a sick struggling lady,
But as a tough, kind, intelligent woman who lasted so long through sickness
And cared about me even though it was hard for her to say so
But I knew she did
And at the time, being there wasn't so scary
I didn't cry then
But now I'm on the verge of tears
And I'm a little scared of the thought
That I saw and touched a dying person
Who was on the road to death
But maybe love made her last a little longer

Days Of My Life

Shabbat

Shabbat is a clear, blue sky, a peaceful, cheery mood that hangs above the world of those who take the time to relax and partake in this holy day.

Shabbat is a classroom, a time that has the opportunity for people to learn about themselves and peace, for peace will be around us during Shabbat, and we will make the time to discover ourselves.

Shabbat is a vacation, a break from everyday life full of rushing and hurries and pains. Along the journey, we will have magical experiences and see beautiful sights.

Shabbat is a reunion, the coziness of being peaceful with family has been separated from us for a week, and we join together with this feeling again for the holy, wondrous day of Shabbat.

Back-to-School

Rushing off the buses,
Greeting old friends,
Chatting in huddles until the bell rings,
Then the new school year begins.

Scrambling to desks,
Labeling bags of supplies,
The scent of new pencils and notebooks linger,
Everything – from shoes to classrooms – are fresh.

Learning the daily routines,
"When is lunch, what day is gym?"
Name games are played to learn bits about each other,
The health and milk and activity notices are passed out.

Leaving the classroom, excited for the year,
Heading home to do first-day homework,
Calling grandparents, they always want to know how school was,
And then the first day has come to an end.

Happy Rosh Hashanah!

Coming together as one family,
"Shanah tova" being said,
Eating apples and honey for the sweetness of life,
And to celebrate the New Year's head.

L'shanah tovah tikateivu, may God write you in the book of life,
Remember and appreciate mitzvot done last year,
And think of the wrong choices you made the previous time,
So you'll know to be more sincere.

Hear the shofar and the joyful songs,
Taste the round challah, it represents the earth,
Happy Rosh Hashanah, the New Year's begun today –
It's the anniversary of our world's birth!

Apples on Rosh Hashanah

Apples are the fruit of knowledge;
We pick them for the new school year.
We hold them in our hands,
They enter our mouths and our minds come autumn
After taking a vacation for the summer,
They are placed on the desks of teachers once again.
Apples are the fruit of knowledge;
We shall eat them in this new year.

Apples are so sweet a fruit
We shall let kindness be harvested along with them for the new year.
Leave the rotten, hateful ones behind on the trees of the past and
Pick the sweet, loving ones for the future.
Hold the apples in our hands,
Put their delicious, pleasure-bringing taste into our mouths,
Let their sweetness and goodness enter our hearts.
Apples are so sweet a fruit;
We shall try to be like them in the new year.

Halloween

Pumpkins on porches,
Phantoms on front yards,
Jack-o-lanterns light the way,
Up to a house,
With witches in windows,
Scarecrows on steps,
You can hear creepy music start to play,
Children dressed up as
Ghosts and green goblins,
And rock stars and princesses too,
They run up to doorsteps,
"May we please have candy,
Thanks so much,
Trick-or-treat to all of you!"
You can hear party music,
Apples are bobbing,
Haunting movies call to be seen,
Inside spooky houses,
The spirits are dancing,
They laugh all night
On Halloween!

Giving on Thanksgiving

Thanksgiving, we are lucky to have such good lives, and now it's time to show our
gratitude,
We gather with our families and give thanks with a positive attitude,
We eat lots of delicious food; we rejoice and sing Thanksgiving songs,
Like the Indians and pilgrims, today we all get along.

Thanksgiving, not only do we show we are grateful for who we are,
We give something to those in need,
By helping, we're each a star,
We have so much and to give our thanks, we go past just saying it in words,
We share our luck with those less fortunate,
We bring celebration to those for whom it has never occurred.

A New Year

A year of life and death has vanished,
Our grandmother, Sylvia, has passed away,
Yet still, we continue to live life in contentment,
And the memory of her will forever stay.

2008 just flew by,
Twelve months have come and past,
A year of laughs, a year of friends and family,
The time has gone so fast.

People cried and people rejoiced,
Acts of kindness and of dread were done,
This year had different meanings for each of us,
In diverse ways, it will be a memorable one.

Come January 20th, a black man will take the president's oath,
That historical election occurred this year,
Although the economy has weakened in the past few months and
Times are not so easy; we still have lots of cheer.

For a new year is a chance to forgive others and start over,
To make up for wrong choices by giving to those in need,
Perhaps all of the people that were nasty and were cruel
Will change in 2009 and do a helpful deed.

But let's forget about the world and the problems in our midst,
We took some great vacations this year and had times of great delight,
In Israel and St. Thomas, at the Greenbrier, Stanford, and the Hamptons,
We enjoyed ourselves each moment, every day and every night.

In the past year, joy and sorrow touched all of our lives,
Exciting and heartbreaking history was made,
In the New Year, we have a chance to change,
We'll replace the wrongs with rights; we'll let the coldness fade.

Valentine's Day

Valentine's day is like a bouquet of roses, many different parts make up its wonder.
The stems of Valentine's Day are the valentines, they only hold it up.
Thanks and love are both the petals, they are what you see and admire most.
But family and friends are the seeds, without them the Valentine's Day Rose would never grow.

Valentine's Day is like a card, each section completes its beauty.
The cover is like red, pink and white hearts, your first impression of Valentine's Day and your first impression of a card.
The white space in the middle is everything to come in our future, moments of beautiful decorations and ones of spilled glue.
The message inside is all of the happiness and enjoyment, for that is really what Valentine's Day means.

Valentine's Day is a special dinner; each course makes it complete and unique.
The appetizers are parties, cookies and other places you go and things you see and do on Valentine's Day.
The main course is hugs and kisses, what fills you up, but it is never complete without the sweet dessert of an "I love you" and the time to remember.
But being with family and friends is the joy of the dinner, just as they are the joy of Valentine's Day.

April Fools!

April 1st – I wake up,
What prank can I play today?
I'll tell my father there's no school, yes,
That's what I will say!

But I will not stop there, no,
I'll make it seem like I'm asleep,
Then I'll sneak out of my room, and my mother –
How she'll freak!

My friends and I write a fake assignment
In a classmate's assignment planner,
My whole class pretends we don't have our math homework,
We behave in a very sneaky manner.

Then, we all go in another classroom to confuse that class,
And on the rug, we sit and write!
As revenge, the teacher sent two boys,
And to worry us, she had them pretend to fight.

After that, we do it again,
We give the students quite a scare!
Then they sneak into our room,
And take all of our chairs!

Our gym teacher tells us we're running,
We're going to do our mile!
We all panic and then we stop,
And give each other smiles.

My friends leave an empty box of Altoids on my desk,
They say they're from someone secret, for me,
Then inside, there's a note:
April Fools! Love from your friend, Lyddie.

We put the box on more desks,
Then when school is let out,
We take two boys' instruments,
And scatter them about.

Later that night, my mother, my sister and I
Take all the sweets out of a junk food drawer,
My dad always goes to get a sweet after dinner,
He's never seen matzah in there before!

It's 6:00 right now,
I've played pranks and received them too,
Still 3 more hours till I go to bed,
Will there be more pranks to receive or do?

Purim

Groggers shaking, making noise,
Lots of dressed up girls and boys.
Hamantaschen flying in the grasp of children's hands,
At so many carnivals, games are played at stands.

Purim schpiels are played, the megillah story is told,
Of Mordechai, so wise, and Esther oh-so-bold,
The joyous day is celebrated with festivities and more,
Out of all the holidays, Purim is never a bore!

The Story of Purim

Vashti refused to go to the dance,
The king said, "I need a new wife,"
Beautiful Esther would be the new queen,
She didn't know how much it would change her life.

Esther was Jewish,
The king didn't know,
To the evil advisor Haman, Esther's cousin Mordechai
Refused to bow down low.

Haman was angry,
He decided to kill all Persia's Jews,
Wise cousin Mordechai said,
"Esther, there must be something you can do."

So Esther was brave,
And she approached the king's throne,
"Ahasverous," she said,
"There's something you must know:"

"I am a Jew, and
Haman has a plot,
He wants to kill us all,"
The king bellowed – "He shall not!"

So evil Haman was hung,
On the gallows he made,
To celebrate this story,
Today, we'll have a parade!

We'll have a carnival; we'll have a party,
We'll make a lot of noise,
And there'll be delicious hamantaschen
For all the girls and boys.

The lesson of this story, well,
I think you may all know,
If you can stand up for yourself and face your fears,
Then you can save your people and be a hero!

Earth Day

Earth Day is a notebook, one little act to help our world done on this day is a word written down that will inspire a great story.

Earth Day is a canvas, one artist willing to paint a picture will start a style of art, called helping the environment.

Earth Day is a New Year's Resolution, after celebrating, when this New Year begins, we will continue to try to keep this resolution, we will try to make our lives filled with Earth Day.

Memorial Day

Memorial Day is a thank you note, sent to veterans who fought for our country, to remind them how much they are appreciated.

Memorial Day is an angel, flying over the veterans that are in the hospital, bringing them comfort and joyous feelings.

Memorial Day is a calling up to the stand, a day when veterans can be honored.

Memorial Day is a flag, a bald eagle, or the Statue of Liberty – like these American symbols, it is a day that shows our patriotism, kindness and respect.

Nature

Butterflies

Flying in the air, like graceful balloons,
Dancing over treetops,
Butterflies.

Beautiful, rainbow wings,
Carrying them just below the clouds,
Delicate, dainty, yet strong,
Butterflies.

Waiting for the group,
Like patient mothers, stopping for their children,
Gorgeous creatures soaring through the sky,
Butterflies.

Winter is . . .
Written with Carly Mazer and Hailey Winterbottom

Winter means to us the beauty of the sparkling snow,
Taking the hats of many snowmen,
The winter wind will blow.

Winter means to us tradition,
Celebrations in the air,
Getting presents, and giving away,
To show that we all care.

Winter means to us hot chocolate, warming us after we play,
Smiles creep on to our faces, it's been a perfect winter day.

Winter means to us sitting with family by the cozy fire light,
Talking and laughing long into
Another winter night.

A Pine Tree

A pine tree is a candle, a pleasant fragrance is always attached, and its strength matches that of the smell.

A pine tree is a sculpture, the base holding it up is the trunk, and the art is the tree, both such unique creations.

A pine tree is a shelter; its needles and branches are wings over anyone who needs a place to stay.

A pine tree is a football player, playing its game in rain or shine.

A pine tree is a decimal, just one little part of a complete forest where each tree works to do a job that can only be done by a whole number.

A pine tree is a wall that flowers may lean on, that will be there for years, until it is time for construction to take place.

A pine tree is a soldier, always in position to defend itself with its sharp needles, always on the lookout for something coming towards it.

A pine tree is a rooftop, sometimes being outlined in frost, and other times turning white from snow.

A pine tree is a family, branching out in generations, staying sturdy and mighty even when the weather is bad, or when times get difficult.

Creek

Slipping through the mountainside,
Bubbling like a boiling pot of water,
Narrow as a small dirt path,
Calm and peaceful is the creek.

Clear water passing towards flat land,
Bumping like a freight train,
Active as an excited child,
Beautiful and intriguing is the creek.

Pebbles hitchhike a wet, rocky ride,
Trees bend down and witness it
Sometimes dipping in for a swim,
People pass and skid to a stop, then watch this water's show,
A magnet to the attention of all,
Proud and talented is the creek.

Snow

Cottonballs parading to the ground,
A closed sign on a school,
Markers coloring the earth white,
A unique and precious jewel.

A switch that makes the whole world freeze,
And makes it quite divine,
A dancer doing a sky show,
Adding magic to all pines.

Confetti falling from the piñata sky,
Sugar that will melt,
A playground for excited kids,
A soft blanket of felt.

Tumbling down to sleep on the grass,
Piling on top of the green,
The wind whistles a lullaby,
Then snow visits another enchanting scene.

The Promise of Spring

Spring promises a summer full of adventures, whether they are around the world or around the corner.

Spring promises stories to be told and reunions to be had with people who have been gone in the winter months.

Spring allows us to unlock the doors we have been trapped in when snow was on the ground and cold was in the air, it allows us to come outside and see the world at its best – to see it in the bloom of spring, with all its promise of an exciting warm weather season.

Spring

Spring parades into our lives on the backs of newborn fuzzy ducklings – quacking cheerfully to say, "Spring is here!"

Spring falls into our world off of the earth-warming sun, bringing heat and sunshine with it.

Spring sprouts from seeds and grows into an exquisite, marvelous flower; each time it is watered and grows, more spring happiness blossoms.

Spring comes out of closets with baseball gear and short sleeves – then it takes over the coats and hats, spring kicking winter out of the world and remaining in the air for a few months.

Spring hatches out of a bird's egg and soon turns into a gorgeous, flying creature called summer.

Storm

The darkening sky with mass clouds of gray,
And the whirling wind go east today,
They stop over us, we dash indoors,
Then the lighting strikes
And the thunder roars!
The drops start like a faucet leaking
They hit the window, streaking
Streaking,
We huddle up,
By the fireplace,
A mix of colors in a case.
The power's gone,
But we don't know,
We're watching the dazzling fire show.
My sister sings,
And we all dance,
The world is forgotten,
We're all in a trance.
Everything bad in the world disappears,
No more sadness, no more fears,
We don't care if we don't have any light,
All we need is the magic, the love on this rainy night.

Spectacular Snowflakes

There are so many wonders in this world,
So many things to see,
A sunset, a butterfly, the patterns in the clouds,
But one is the most spectacular to me.

Snowflakes fall and cover the ground
There are feet and feet of white,
And when one lands on my dark glove
It brings me great delight.

It has a beautiful pattern,
Some exquisite criss-crossed lines,
And then another one lands on my glove,
And I have an amazing find.

It's equally incredible, yes it is,
But it's not the same at all,
It's diversely patterned and shaped,
Then on the ground it falls.

Two things so different are both so gorgeous,
Then they mix in with the snow on the ground,
Each individual, fine snowflake
Is nowhere to be found?

They're both working together,
To cover the ground in white,
When I wake up the next morning and think how many beautiful snowflakes are
blanketing the earth,
It's an even more amazing sight.

So why are snowflakes the most wondrous thing,
Out of all the wonders I've ever seen?
They're so different and all so beautiful
And they work together to make a spectacular snow scene.

Deer

One in the morning, alone and timid,
Looks up at me from the lawn.
Sees my face pressed against the window, looking at her,
Looks away, stays awhile, rubs against a tree,
Darts off.
Two in the afternoon, shy ones,
But two of them! A pair!
Is it the same deer from the morning?
Or is it two friends, or perhaps mother and baby, or husband and wife?
They dare to cross our backyard, but as soon as they see my face pressed against the
window, looking at them, they dart off.
The first deer, alone, not confident to come onto the grass, yet brave enough to stay,
even though I was there.
The second deer, bold enough to be on our grass,
A pair of them, who dash off as soon as our eyes meet.
Is that how loners are, unsure at first and then confident when they have a friend?
Is that how pairs are, daring but when there is a third one, afraid of the content duo
being split or harmed?

When the Wind Picks Up

The leaves jump off the ground,
Like it burns them.
They settle down again.
The branches on trees rustle, then,
They become still again.
The wind is blowing, but only gently, only gently,
Then it picks up again.

The leaves leap up into the sky,
Circling around, curving around everywhere in the air like a hurricane, the cyclone of
leaves gyrating around overhead,
Going up and down, all around, up and down again.
The bare branches rub against each other, and then start to shake in the wind, they
move side-to-side, side-to-side, and side-to-side again.
The wind blows the world, whistling and huffing and puffing,
People's clothes wave back and forth, little children try to keep their feet on the
ground,
"Don't blow away! Don't blow away!"

Then, the leaves stop whirling around, and they return to the ground again.
The branches stop shaking and the trees settle down again.
The wind stops howling, it ceases in its blowing of the world, of its huffing and puffing
and shaking, until it picks up again.

Autumn's Taste of Winter

Sleeping children lay still in their beds, warm and cozy; the temperature
Has dropped since evening and the evening is cooler than the day;
Each week there is more of a chill in the air, every day stronger winds send down cold
from the sky.
When morning comes, dew drops on the grass, and the frigid weather trickles down a
visual sign that it is here on the earth. What it sends down to the ground from the sky
is not yet a snow, but a frost.
The children peer out the window sleepily, and see the grass decorated in white frost,
They gather at the bus stop, hats and mittens on for the first time this season.
Kids take many breaths from their mouths, watching a cloud appear and fade away
into the chill of the day. The bus rides past a thinly iced pond, past grasses that look
like they are drizzled with sugar crystals; scarecrows set up for Halloween wish they
had sweaters, shivering in the frosty air; pumpkins grow frost on them too, sitting on
stoops during Autumn's taste of winter.

Winter's Taste of Spring

When the children wake up, they expect another cold day,
Their mothers warn them that it may be warmer today – they will not need heavy coats,
Some children listen, others don't – those who do not listen will regret it.
The morning feels like all the other days – perhaps a bit sunnier, but it isn't
dramatically different. The day in school is normal too, until recess.
For the first time in a long time, recess is outdoors,
The children are warned to stay out of the melted remains of the February slush, and
they expect it to be chilly – but they are in for a surprise,
When they step onto the playground, the hot sun beats down on them,
All of their coats go off, and for those in winter clothes, it is uncomfortably hot, even
though it is only 60 degrees.
Everyone goes outside to be in the comfortably warm weather,
Snowmen who wish to see July are unlucky - they will melt before they
Get a chance to meet March.
Even though it won't last long, people enjoy being in the fresh air during winter's taste
of spring.

Moods of the Months, Sense of the Season
A Poem about The Different Months of Winter

The frigid wind pushes brittle, auburn October leaves off into the empty roads, making way for the frost. The thin, delicate coat of ice settles down on the grass, giving the green lawns a sheer, frosty tint. Children can see their breath, forming a small cloud outside in the chilly air. A wintry mood fills the atmosphere; autumn is forgotten for a little while as the world gets a preview of winter.

Children glare outside, filled with excitement as the first snow begins to fall. It does not stick to the ground, but a few flakes drizzle down from the heavens. The children dash to the windows of the classrooms, all peering out, praying for the snow to stick. The flakes melt as soon as they hit the ground as they remember it is only November, but everyone is energized at the brief visit of snow.

Each December morning the children dart to the windows and press their faces against them, fogging up the windowpanes with their breath. They look for signs of snow, and finally, there are patches of white covering the grass. It is not enough for a snow day; the ground is not yet sleeping under a completely white blanket, but still the children buzz about the small patches of snow, covering over little bits of the freezing ground.

Heaps of snowflakes pile up over the grass – there is not a trace of green. The bare trees are coated, cars are transformed white, and the roofs of buildings have icicles hanging off the sides and flurry on the tops. School is canceled and children sled down hills all day, building joyful snowmen and having friendly snowball fights. The magical white world is harmless and peaceful; it seems as if everyone is happy in the January blizzard.

The gloomy gray sky hangs over the world in late February; the wonder of winter has ceased and all of the snow becomes mucky slush. Cars are no longer covered in magical white snow, they are splashed with mud and sludge and slip and slide in the yuckiness of the leftover snow. Although everything is so sorrowful and the weather is nasty – there is no more enchanting winter feeling – all of the children know that the slush will soon go away and there will be the beauty of spring and the enjoyment of summer ahead, and then another winter will soon be on its way, beginning with the October frost, then the November flakes, then the December flurry, then the January blizzards.

Ideas And Emotions

Seven Miles

Here, in Short Hills, I have little to worry about.
Mostly I only worry about too much homework
Or something difficult we're studying in school
Or maybe a piano song I'm having trouble with.

Here – it's simple.
There's just always enough food.
If we run out, we go to the supermarket.
Here, we have drawers and closets, bursting with clothes.
If we need more, we just go to the store.

Seven miles.
It doesn't seem like very far.
It might take me a little more than an hour to jog seven miles.
It takes about fifteen minutes to drive that far.

But seven miles away is a different world.

People in tattered clothes live in the streets, or run down homes.
They have little food.
They have little hope.

Here – in Short Hills,
We cry because of sentimental little things.
Moving on.
Growing up.
Time flying.
Maturing.

There – just seven miles away,
Childhood doesn't fade away, in ceremonies and tears.

No.
There, childhood is stripped away from you.
Yanked, grabbed out of your hands as a toddler.
Eight and nine year olds care for their two and three year old brothers and sisters.
They roam the streets – parentless.

Is this really just seven miles?
At one end, we have too much?
At the other, they have nothing?

Yes. This is just seven miles.
And we travel the seven miles.
We travel them.
And give them a little bit.
But the miles still seem far.
Let's build a bridge and make them closer.
Spread it all just seven miles.
Build a bridge between those two worlds.

Comfort is . . .

Comfort is an angel, coming down to make sure you're safe.

Comfort is a light, leading you back home.

Comfort is a voice, telling you you're not all alone.

Comfort is a simple touch, to feel the company of a friend by your side.

The Forms of Wonder

Wonder can fall down from the sky in winter, in the form of white flakes that each have unique shapes. It can coat the trees in exquisiteness and cover the ground with a magical blanket.

Wonder can faintly be seen in the sky when the sun is out but rain still falls. It can arch over the world in a mixture of colors, and the glimpses caught of it will be treasured forever by its viewers.

Wonder can spill pink paint over the clouds on a tranquil summer evening and turn the sky orange and purple. It can pull the vast, dazzling sun down and bring up a full moon, glimmering in the black, cloud-free emptiness of the night. Then a new wonder takes place, the brilliant shining of hundreds of stars, dancing into the forms of many miraculous constellations, wonder filling up the sky.

Death

Death is a cloud of grief,
Filling up the sky.

Death is a tear, there will
Always be times when it trickles
Down your face in memory.

Death is a moving van, bringing
A soul up to the heavens, to have
Another person care for us.

Death is a spark of hope, when
There is death; there will be life.

Playfulness

If playfulness were a color,
It would be sky blue – a color so bright and without troubles.
If playfulness were a taste,
It would be just like crunchy cookies, an entertaining, sweet taste just like playfulness
is.
If playfulness were a feeling
It would be as hilly as a rocky mountain with many bumps of laughter and games.
If playfulness were a smell,
It would smell as fresh and crisp as clear ocean water – an easygoing and carefree scent
just like playfulness.
If playfulness were a sound,
It would be as strong and loud as wind chimes, ringing in my ear so proudly, as
independent and cheerful as playfulness.

A Borderless World

God, up in the heavens,
Looked at earth and claimed it good.
No boundaries, all open.
No lines of separation of peoples,
Just land and water.
And when Adam and Eve had a boundary –
The Forbidden Fruit –
That was when the world's troubles began.

People closing out, creating boundaries,
Leads to hurt feelings.
"You can't. You're not good enough.
You're not one of us. We're better than yous"
Lead to anger and tears.

When countries create boundaries,
Of land and of ethnicities and races,
Blood is shed and lives are taken.

From the heavens, God doesn't see these boundaries,
These lines of territory and ranking,
God's perspective of the world is lineless,
We should erase all of these lines
And make the world the way God sees it.

A Better World

I wish I could help make world peace,
I wish no one would ever tease.
I wish we all could understand,
I wish all nations would join hands.

I wish the world a better place,
I wish for fairness between every race,
I wish for education, homes and healthcare for all,
I wish no one would make others bawl.

I wish to discover, to learn all new facts,
I wish I could accomplish so many great tasks,
I wish the world were always clean,
I wish we'd all decide to go green!

I wish I were better at things such as sports,
I wish one day there would be peace for people of all sorts,
I wish that no one would make others sad,
I wish for all these wishes to come true, although already, my life's not bad.

Running

Gracefully dashing,
Jogging continuously,
Free, in my own world.

A Prayer of Inspiration

Eternal God, open up my lips so my mouth may declare Your glory.

Eternal God, unclench my fists so my hands can reach out to others.

Eternal God, inspire us to pray, so we can sing of your brilliance and splendor.

Eternal God, make me b'tzelem elohim, teach me to do mitzvot like You, and I will fix the world that You created.

Inspire us to pray to You, Adonai.
After You hear us worshipping You, You will know that we put our trust in You, and we will devote our lives to keeping Your earth safe.

Yet we still need inspiration to go out and do mitzvot, to make the world a better place. Be our teacher, Adonai, and we will be Your faithful students. If You make us b'tzelem elohim – in Your image – then we will promise to use this title for good and keep our promise to dedicate our lives to improving Your world.

After you have inspired us to pray to you, and you have realized we are forever loyal to you and protecting your earth, after you have inspired us to fulfill our promises and taught us how to go out and do mitzvot, then make us b'tzelem elohim – like you, Eternal God, for you are peaceful, and unclench our fists, so our hands can reach out to others.

Then, we will continue to keep our promise to be b'tzelem elohim, and like you did for us, oh God, we will unclench the fists of the poor, we will unclench the fists of the evil, we will unclench the fists of those who destroy the world, and their hands will reach out to others.

You must light the inspirational fire, and we will carry it around the world on a torch. Be our inspiration to do good, and we will do so, and then pass the inspiration around.

The History of Everyday Life

American history, compiled into a textbook.
Hundreds of years, into a hundred or so pages.
What makes it in?
Wars, inventions,
Events and people who left a big enough footprint that
it still remains today.

But – what is left out?

Did little girls miss their daddies who fought in the Continental Army?
Did teenagers during the Civil War all want to go to the same types of parties,
Whether they were slaves or owners?

After all, these are the things that make up childhood.
These are the troubles and joys that are really the whole worlds of children.
Compared to inventions and laws and wars,
This is unimportant.
But after all, these make up our country's history too – don't they?

So, are all the parties we go to
And the games we play
And the emotions we have forgotten?
They are unimportant?

No, that is not true.
And anyone who truly wants to know about history
Will dig that deep and answer these questions.
They'll go beyond the textbooks
And find out what life was really like.

As for us, we're just a little blip
On the scheme of time and history.
Will we be remembered? And, for what?
If we don't make a footprint
Big enough to be seen throughout the world,
Will the memories of us be lost?

If no one is willing to dig deep enough and find our footprints, covered with dust,
Then – yes.
But if a person really wants to know
And digs very far, then the footprints of the past will be seen again.

The Blind Man

The hustle and bustle of the city
The cabs on the street
The streets filled with stands
The shops
The lights of Broadway.

The blind man roams the street
With a cane for eyes
He can't see the cabs
The stands on the street
The shops
The lights of Broadway.

The blind man can only guess
What the city looks like.
He can find the streets and the sidewalks
And he knows when he is at the subway
For he can hear the trains rolling in
And he can feel the raised bumps on the ground.

So the blind man can hear, and he can feel
He can taste all the food in the restaurants
He can smell hot dogs on the street
So although the blind man can't see the city,
He can still sense it.

The blind man can't see the city,
So he can't judge it by appearance either.
If someone is unattractive,
The blind man doesn't know.
There's so much prejudice against color and race in this world,
And all because of sight.

We depend too much on our eyes,
We have five senses for a reason.
If the blind man can still get around the city,
Without seeing and partaking in its prejudice,
Maybe we'd all be better off blind.
Maybe, he's actually lucky.

Time

Sometimes minutes whiz by,
Where did they all go?
Sometimes hours and days escape us,
Other times, time seems so slow.

When you're anticipating news or a very special day,
All of the time leading up to it seems to drag,
Watching the seconds tick by, oh when will the bell ring?
When will the mail come? Every millisecond seems to lag!

Yet when this day that you are waiting for finally arrives,
The minutes disappear; time really seems to fly,
Before you know it, there'll be something else
That you so badly want to come,
But in the mean time, each second lingers,
Each moment is humdrum.

The Satisfaction of Silence

From a piano, a melodious tune rings,
A vibrant, cheery bird resting in a tree sings,
Waterfalls rush down into tranquil, refreshing creeks,
A kind mother, gentle and loving, holds her baby, and tenderly speaks.

Yet in the composition, the notes stop – a rest appears,
And the bird flies away to catch a worm and the whistling sound disappears,
The baby falls asleep and the mother starts to silently knit,
The sounds were all so pleasant, but sometimes we need quiet.

Ocean waves are crashing, and then they wash up ashore,
Raindrops patter on the roof – but inside you're secure,
These sounds are all so lovely, but when the storms stop, we're still content,
Sometimes we have an urge for serenity, which can bring us wonderment.

A concert performed by an orchestra is always a delightful sound,
Yet sometimes everywhere you look, the noise is all around,
Being sucked into a world of bangs and booms may make us have a fit,
And then we crave the magic called silence – even if it's just for a minute.

When the world is silent we can make time briefly freeze,
We can be alone in solitude and think whatever we please,
We can dream up the impossible and make plans to do great things,
And once we've done all this – we've had our fill of silence – the world, once again, sings.

Laughter

Little girls giggling and gushing with grins full of glee,
Tiny babies gurgling when there's something astounding that they see,
Children chortling at a joke or a hilarious tale,
Grandpas guffawing, bursting with laughter, they soon need to stop and exhale.

Titters and sniggers, ha-has and hee-hees,
Chuckles, hoots, and cackles at humorous comedies,
The whole world is filled with laughter, and it all sounds one-of-a-kind,
Like there are many kinds of laughs, there are different types of people you will find.

There are the giggles, so different from all of the hoots,
The hoots are not from small children, they are louder, stronger, less cute,
The giggles are quieter; they are from adorable young girls,
This represents the people of the world – each has different traits – finding out what
they are can take you on a whirl.

For if you don't know that a cackle most likely intends to be cruel,
And you trust all the cackling people; you could wind up in a duel,
If you suspect that a gurgle is harmful, then you've got a lot to learn,
Like laughs, people are different, some are trustworthy, but others may betray you,
Those cackles may turn.

So like laughs, people are unique from one another,
Some are more honest than some others,
In the world, we all must know which laughs to trust,
We have to know which ones can't be our friends; we have to stick with the ones that we
know must.

String

The straight spine of a soldier
At attention.

Under its skin, the intricate, miniscule
Systems of a
Braided
Human body.

The end, an old building,
Frayed and chipped
By the years of its use.

A gymnast, able to bend her body,
To twist it and wrap it around.

A smooth-faced, soft skinned baby.

A puppy. It can easily get into a
KNOT of trouble!

Purple

Lavender
Brings calmness
A floating
Cheery feel
Deep purple
Brings royalty
Hope
Richness
Fullness
A jeweled queen
Violet
Joyful energy
Bouncing
Happy
Fun
Purple
Conveyor of calmness
Pulls people
To the sky
I feel like I can float
So cheery
Hopeful
Complete
Peaceful
I'm a queen
Bouncing
Joyful
Happiness
Fun
When I wear
Purple

Music

Music is more than sounds arranged
To please the human ear,
Music is a hand to turn a switch
Of emotions you never knew you had.
Music can jerk tears out of your eyes
In just a simple melody and soothing words,
Music can blow you up like a bubble of happiness,
Floating into a cheery sky,
And sometimes, music can make you forget all your troubles,
And just make you want to dance,
Music can hold the answers to your problems,
If you listen carefully enough,
Music can put more than a picture in your mind,
But a beautifully, uniquely colored emotion,
Music can open you up to be a person that you never knew was inside.

Why?

Why must we be jealous? Why must we want what others have?
Why can't we be grateful for how lucky we are?
Why do we take our world for granted?
Why do we not appreciate how good our lives are?
Why do we always want them to be better?

Why must we fight?

Why can't we stop and think oh –
How amazing this all is! –
Even when times seem tough?

Why can we never be happy?
Why can't we be satisfied with the little things?

Why don't we all hold hands, in peace,
and sing songs of giving
and kindness
and friendship
and joy?
It isn't that simple, they say.
But why?

Happiness

I am a river,
Flooding with happiness!
Smiles pour out of me,
Kindness flows from my hands and my mouth,
For I am overflowing with happiness,
Glee swims throughout me,
If only it could swim through everyone!

I know that some people
May be experiencing droughts,
Maybe there is nothing for glee to swim in inside them,
Well, don't worry,
I've got enough happiness water to spread cheer around!

I know I'm lucky to be flooding,
I feel bad for rivers that are dry,
For those that have nothing,
For those who are empty of reasons for cheer,
Those that never learned optimism,
But instead of letting my surplus water
Just run away in waste,
I'll save it in a bucket
To spread to those waterless rivers,
I'll pass the happiness around!

Then maybe one day,
Our world will have many more rivers,
The earth will flood with happiness
And smiles
And kindness
And maybe it will be because
I overflowed with happiness,
And passed the water on.

Diversity

I feel like I am floating,
All my troubles drift away,
Nothing can bring me down –
I feel good today!

Free as a little bird,
Up, away I'll fly!
But how is it that some days,
I just want to cry?

Some days, the sky is gloomy,
The whole world just seems bad,
I want to be alone,
Be sucked in by all my mad.

Well, we could never have the happy,
If we didn't have the sad.
It would all just seem the same –
Insipid, plain and drab.

Candies – oh, so sweet!
Chocolates – so delicious!
But some food is disgusting,
Bland, pukish – nutritious.

But candy would just be normal
If everything tasted sweet.
It would just be average food,
No longer a yummy treat.

So we need a little diversity,
A balance of good and bad,
'Cause we'd never appreciate happiness
If there was nothing sad.

Plane Perspective

As the plane soars into the air,
The raindrops on the window whoosh away.
Where do they go?
They are whisked off into eternity,
Left to the sky,
Evaporating into thin air.
The sky has warped the raindrops
Spiraled them off into the sky.
These drops are not the same as raindrops on the ground
The wetness fades
The air makes them vanish away.

Clouds, from the ground, look puffy,
Thick, impossible to push through,
Yet in the sky the clouds part for the plane
They are a thin cloth, spreading, spreading
Thin and sheer
A curtain of mist
The sky has changed the perspective
Spun and stretched the clouds out
The sky has made them diaphanous mist that parts for the way of the plane.

And up from the sky, the houses and trees look so small
So little, so unimportant
Yet I realize
All of these houses are someone's life
They may just be tiny dots from a plane
But they shape the existence of a person's life
The plane has warped the houses
The perspective of their importance
The sky has made them look small.

Back on the ground again
The raindrops stay
The clouds are thick
The houses and trees are big and important again
The sky has not warped these things
Only shifted the perspective.

The sky has taught me something.
There's not always a right or a wrong answer,
There's not necessarily bad or good
There's just a transferal of view
Nothing's really changed.

Hope

I swing my racquet and miss,
It lands in the net,
So many times,
The little balls don't make it,
They go to a cemetery at the net,
If I miss so many shots,
Why do I keep swinging?

The leaf blowers escort the leaves into piles,
Wind tries to free them again,
Wind is more powerful,
The leaves scatter,
But the leaf blowers return.
Why do they always try to tame the leaves,
When they know wind will let them loose?

So many Jews – killed in the Holocaust.
Six million.
Wiped out.
Gone.
When so many of us have died,
How do we still have that hope?
That little piece of hatikvah
When we have lost lives, lost battles,
How is hatikvah still here?

Maybe it's magic. Hope.
It seems unrealistic – strange and miraculous that we believe in it.
But I swing and hope that ball will go over the net.
And when it does, I know the power of hope.

Without hope,
Jews would not be here today.
Israel would not be here today.
We would have given up years ago without hope.
The streets of Israel are built from hope,
From hatikvah,
And that's why we always must believe in
This magical, miraculous, unrealistic
Vital hope –
It's what keeps us all standing.

Billisecond

It's amazing that there's something as short as a billisecond,
By the time that you counted to one,
Millions would have gone by.
Nothing happens in a billisecond. Everything happens in a billisecond.
What difference does a billisecond make? None. All.
Terror takes a billisecond to strike.
Joy takes a billisecond to be had.
A battle, a birth,
It wouldn't be the same without a billisecond.
Our earth would be so different if you took away a few billiseconds!
Still, by the time you counted to a billisecond,
Millions would have gone by.
As I write this poem,
Trillions have gone by.

Climbing Over my Worries of Fear

My hands creeping up each rock,
Legs trembling,
Me, about to cry in nervousness.
I was so far up the wall,
But there were mountains of space under me.
I could fall so far if my shaking hand slipped.
Yet the chain and harness were magnets,
Attached to the metal me.
Even though it was their fault that I dangled
In space when I attempted to escape to solid ground,
The chain and harness kept me safe from sinking, sinking
And falling.
As I finally reach the top, so proud and joyous,
The chain jingles and Mommy's claps and cheers
Roar and strike like a storm.
Yet as I begin to climb the second wall,
It seems like it is at the top of the earth.
I cry and whisper, "I want to come down."
And my wish is granted.
This endeavor brings fear and worries of fear,
Yet there is no need to be scared of fear,
For I am safe,
There is no need to be anxious.
Finally, it is time to go,
A feeling of sore accomplishment
Passes over me like a sudden wind.
Today I always smile when I
Remember this adventure.
My new hope is to rock climb again,
So I can conquer the small walls more easily,
And with joy,
And make it to the top of the second wall,
For there is no reason to be afraid.

Holding Hands

A mother holds a child's hand
While crossing the street,
Friends hold hands
As they run across a playground,
A couple holds hands too.

A sign of protection
A sign of friendship
A sign of love
Is holding hands.

We hold hands with those we are close to.
We hold hands with our friends,
With those we care about
With those we love.
And that is okay.

We are comfortable holding hands with those people,
It is soothing,
Enjoyable,
It makes us feel loved.

But not everyone has a hand to hold.
Those are the people we should extend our arms to,
Reach out for,
Even if we do not feel comfortable doing so.

Imagine a world where everyone holds hands.
Everyone is protected
Everyone has friends
Everyone is loved.
Reach out and hold a hand.
You'll help to make it so.

The Keys to the World

Art is a key to the world,
Colors, textures and shapes are brushed onto canvas,
The way blank paper is transformed,
The way wonders are recreated with paints,
Beauty is formed,
The door is open.

Music is a key to the world,
Fingers pressing on keys, strumming guitars, beating drums,
The way tones come from instruments,
The way songs come from notes,
A melodious tune rises,
The door is open.

Words are a key to the world,
Opening the dictionary to find just the right ones to describe amazing sensations,
The way letters are put together to create words, to create images,
The way each one sounds and means something unique,
How words are blocks to build a writing tower,
A poem is written,
The door is open.

Friendship is a key to the world,
People, all diverse, come together to laugh and celebrate,
The way friends can trust each other,
The way true friends are friends forever,
Special bonds are created,
The door is open.

Optimism is a key to the world,
Keeping a smile on your face no matter what,
The way you can always think on the bright side,
The way every gray cloud has a cheery silver lining,
Sunshine can overpower at least a little of the gloom,
The door is open.

Happiness is a key to the world,
Knowing that there's at least one little thing that's good about your life,
Or that someone loves you, or you make someone else happy,
The way we can always turn to something, no matter how small and taken for granted it is,
When we are gloomy,
The fact that we have a world to live on, and that there is even such a thing as art, music,
words, friendship, optimism, and happiness on our earth, is enough to make me happy,
If the little things can make everyone happy,
And we can spread the cheer,
Then the door will be unlocked – but we have to open it ourselves.

The Hands of a Writer

Grasping pencils,
Stretching fingers across the page,
The messenger of the mind's ideas,
The hands of a writer.

Touching lessons,
Producers of rich, clear visions,
Teachers, forming beauty to learn,
The hands of a writer.

Dancing moves – the letters,
Each ballerina does a dance of a story,
Actresses, entertaining the audience watching the play,
The hands of a writer.

The Writer's Process

When a poem comes to my head
It's like fresh dough –
If I touch on it too much,
The baked bread won't be delicious!
I have to get it out
Or else
I will
EXPLODE!

The little poem thought particles
Evolve and fill me up with thoughts
Thoughts that isolate me
Drown out the life and fun
And fill me with deep thoughts.
And questions and whys
And the answer is always
WRITE.

Write, write, write, write, write.
I HAVE TO WRITE!

And if I don't write,
Then
I will
EXPLODE!

I have to write fast
Or else I'll have wasted precious time I could be enjoying
By deciding I should write!

But I know that already.
Because I am a writer.
And, a writer always writes.

Courtney Cooperman is a twelve year old girl who has been writing poetry since second grade. She is publishing her poetry book to raise money for her bat mitzvah service project. Besides writing, Courtney also loves to play piano, read, spend time with friends, play softball, run, play tennis, and do charity projects. Courtney lives with her parents and sister in Short Hills, New Jersey and attends Millburn Middle School. She is so excited to have her book published and eager to share her poems.